THE SECRET OF AN OPTIMISTIC MIND

5 steps to creating and enjoying a full life

THE SECRET OF AN OPTIMISTIC MIND

5 steps to creating and enjoying a full life

By Léa Liger

Translated from French by Rosemary Milne

e-Book cover design and layout formatting by Obrad Vukojević, odizajn.com

Contact

contact@optim-etre.com, www.optim-etre.com

contact@secretofoptimism.com

Layout formatting and distribution of the book by

www.ebook-creation.fr

ISBN: 978-2-9556384-0-8

© 2016, Léa Liger

TABLE OF CONTENTS

ABOUT THE AUTHOR

Léa Liger founded 'Optim-Etre' which trains people to proactive and optimistic thinking through coaching and meditation. She previously practiced trade law for more than twenty years with a government agency.

As a consultant, a Neuro-Linguistic-Programming (NLP) practitioner and certified coach, Léa runs seminars and lectures on self-discovery and skills development. She has guided educational organizations in transition periods to define and realize their projects, based on the Appreciative Inquiry Approach. She has conducted and run long-term projects of adult training programs in France and Europe for 15 years, centred on life skills and interpersonal skills. She has written a book on Values and Education *"Projet Educatif - Expériences et Méthodes"* and has had papers published in several specialized magazines. Her main interest is to promote a positive approach to change and challenges and to help people rekindle their dreams to make them become true.

INTRODUCTION

These days, when we are being constantly bombarded by bad news from all parts of the media, the best way to protect ourselves is to cultivate an optimistic frame of mind. The optimist is someone who looks on the bright side (the half-full glass) and who is sufficiently hopeful about the future to be prepared to act and to undertake new projects. A further benefit of optimism is that it enables us to see, beyond the present difficulties or challenges (the half-empty glass), the possibility of positive outcomes in the future. If we can maintain such an attitude the fear of loss is replaced by excitement at the possibility of a new start.

It follows from this that if we wish to remain optimistic, no matter how problematic the circumstances, it is essential to understand our thought processes and the quality of the thoughts created by those processes. Our natural optimism is just waiting to be unleashed. Optimism and pessimism are two sides of the same coin, the front side showing a radiant smile and the reverse the price we pay for worrying too much.

In fact, nothing happens by chance. We make choices and those choices are based on our understanding of how we construct our reality and that in turn is largely influenced by cultural and linguistic patterns. This means that in order to explore this question further, we must consider certain characteristics of Western languages that have shaped the European world view and to do that we must begin by looking back at the origins of the European languages.

Many centuries ago in Greece, a new class of merchants and craftsmen became greatly interested in establishing peace in the territories with which they were building trade links. But a question arose: What is peace? What conditions are required to guarantee stable exchanges between countries with different practices and customs?

- To appreciate the difficulty, you can think about the ideas that occur to you when you think of the word 'peace'. Do you think everyone has the same definition of it? Does it not

change according each individual's experience, cultural or political background?

The Greeks decided that the best way of ensuring there were no conflicts or wars would be to prevent them in the first place, and to do this what was required were methods for settling disputes. First and foremost, those rules or methods had to be subject to the approval of all stakeholders. This realization triggered debate about choosing the appropriate rules and principles. The debates took place in a public square named the Agora and involved all the notable thinkers of the city. The Agora is still remembered as the place where the foundations of today's democracy were laid.

For the first time in the recorded history of mankind, the inherited explanation of the world through Mythos had to yield to a more objective and functional understanding of how reality operates. The function of myths is to explain symbolically how the world - matter and mankind - is created, and to depict the play of natural forces on the human condition. Founding myths belong to pre-rational thought, whereas the upcoming Logos can be submitted to the test of reason and the search for truth.

When they undertook this work, those Greek thinkers had to be realistic in their search for effective solutions. There were two main tools which they used to work out a set of stable general principles: a spirit of observation and a powerful practice of reflective and critical thinking. Together these helped them to understand how to relate one fact to another, one behaviour to another in order to establish the rules by which to govern the people. The same process gave birth to philosophy and laid the foundations of the scientific mind.

This process required the ancient Greeks to search for the essence of phenomena, setting to one side subjective factors such as moods, emotions, social characteristics or levels of education as well as any short-, medium- or long-term change to the condition and content of the observed phenomena. By this means they discovered timeless reason, Logos, that belongs only to itself. "Logos or abstract thinking does not reside in nature, it belongs to language," noted

Jean-Pierre Vernant, a French specialist in the field of Greek philosophy.

I can say from experience that logic has its limits, especially when it is focused on the outside world of phenomena. As a graduate of a Business School and of the prestigious Sorbonne University in Paris, I was steeped in this cultural mind-set as a result of my many years of study of management, law, linguistics and literature. But nothing in all that I learned taught me how to deal with my inner reality when I found myself in difficult and upsetting situations.… Even studying theories of the emotions was of no help. Two factors changed my life. The first was discovering Neuro-Linguistic Programming (N.L.P.) which helped me to change my inner conversation - moving away from abstract language to focused clear dialogue. This transformed my inner reality; providing me strength and pleasure. The second was meditation. The regular practice of Raja Yoga meditation during 30 years was critical in developing the subtle, creative dimensions of my 'neglected' mind. The combined effect of these two methods produced quite startling results: I was energised, more fully alive and aware of my creative potential and my innate worth than I had ever been before.

CHAPTER I

Constructing Reality

"How is it that humans have progressed so rapidly in science, mathematics, and engineering, yet we continue to exhibit behaviours that result in misunderstanding, suspicion, bigotry, hatred, and even violence in our dealings with other people and with other cultures?"- Alfred Korzybski

I - The cultural background

Korzybski's statement, made at the close of the First World war, is obviously still valid. As has been said, every day the media provide proof that, despite the civilizing effects of reason, irrationality and conflict remain the norm throughout the world. Why is that? One of the prime causes is our thought processes which have shaped our culture and world view, our "weltanschauung".

In 1933, Alfred Korzybski, an Austrian engineer, wrote *'Science & Sanity; an Introduction to Non-Aristotelian Systems and General Semantics'*, in which he presented his view of the role of language in the perceptual process.

Korzybski noted that the structures of language that determine how we think are not only no longer adapted to contemporary science, they do not meet the needs of modern man in general. Unlike mathematics and science which use symbols to explain the facts observed, *"those who build social, economic, political structures use languages (ideas and approaches) inherited from pre-scientific, mythological, metaphysical dogmas"*. This means not only that errors are introduced, but that those errors can result in conflicts of catastrophic proportions, such as the "First World War". The general semantic Korzybski invented was designed to fit the modern world and human nature of today, not that of Aristotle's era, 350 years before Christ.

Most of us have been reared and educated in this language. We use it in our daily lives. That is why this idea concerns every one of us.

Aristotle founded logic as a science by establishing a comprehensive inventory and classification of the natural elements that are accessible to sensory perception. He said nature can be divided in two groups : non-living things (stones, water, soil) that can only be modified by an external act, and living things, endowed with the capacity to transform themselves. Living things themselves can be divided into two groups: plants and living beings. This last group includes species (cow, horse, bird, fish…) and human beings whose defining characteristic is the faculty to think, that is to say to classify our sense impressions into different groups and categories.

The Middle Ages rediscovered Aristotle's work, whose influence became dominant in European universities and schools from that time on, and has remained so until today. Twenty centuries later, we recognize that by using increasingly abstract reasoning we can speed up communication, expand our mental space to elaborate more sophisticated scientific or ethical thinking, as well as to establish the rules and regulations governing a city.

The entire progression from reliance on the experience of the five senses to the acquisition of the capacity to name things, is fundamental to the development of any adult and civilization, and essential in the growth of the individual from childhood to adulthood. It is an essential part of the process of individuation, to use the term coined by Carl Gustav Jung.

II - The structure of language

Coming back to Alfred Korzybski's study on the Aristotelian structure of language, he underlined three main points that have conditioned the European mind since the Middle Ages. These three points have shaped our perceptions, restricting our mental processes, as we shall see.

- The use of the verb 'to be'

There is one main verb in Indo-European languages: the verb 'to be'. It is used in four different ways, two of which have no major influence on our thinking: we can say without ambiguity *"this is finished"* using 'is' as an auxiliary of the verb to finish. Likewise, we can use it as a verb of existence: I am, (I exist).

However, the two other uses of 'to be' are more problematic. They affect us more personally because they determine our perception of ourselves as well as our relationship with nature, with our fellow men and events. Used in this way, they impact on our self-image and self-esteem.

- To be, a verb designating an identity

'A rose is a flower', 'a poplar is a tree', are statements of identity.

"I am a woman" presents problems of a different order, especially if you consider the status of women in some parts of the globe. It appears to be a straightforward, quick description of oneself but it is far from satisfactory, since it does not define the essential 'me'.

- What is the sum total of all the identities you embody during a day, a week, a year or years: a consultant, a manager, an employee, a woman/man, a wife/husband, a mother/father, a musician, a sportsman, etc.?

- Can you think of one all-encompassing identity which truly sums up all these different facets of yourself? You are the person thinking of all these identities. If you can think of them, it must mean you are distinct from them. You have

created them. They are parts of you. So, who are you? You are the conscious being, the creator of your behaviour and actions. You have the power to create your life and your roles and to assume them fully… or to relinquish them if they no longer suit you.

The concept of identity becomes less clear when we are emotionally implicated in a situation. Whether you see yourself as a manager or an employee, the person who is your superior has authority over you and the job you are responsible for is based on a contract of some kind, which in turn requires you to produce certain agreed results (productivity, cash flow...). If you see yourself as an overstretched employee, facing these two external realities, (the authority of the manager and the demands of the contract), you will be faced with three unconnected 'realities', all of them based on what is required of you, i.e. what is your duty or your responsibility. You are not expected to be engaged emotionally in your job, but the fact is that you are. The effect of this is that you will either project onto the task or onto your manager your desire for recognition, your fear of failure and your rejection of control, and these feelings will add further to the confusion in your emotional landscape.

- A more satisfactory approach is to imagine you are on a stage and YOU are an actor playing a role in a 'bigger picture' drama called life. Seen this way, the scope of the game becomes much wider and the new enlarged context provides you with more possibilities. You are an actor, but so is your boss, and both of you are playing out a scenario. Make it as good as you can. The position you hold at work is your individual participation in work which is being carried out all over the globe. Thinking of it in this way allows us to introduce some humanity into the game. Nevertheless, the game remains a game.

- What might you do or say and using what kind of tone in that game?

- How does your manager answer? How do you feel?

The image you have of yourself is paramount in shaping your happiness and your success. Depending on your attitude to human evolution, you may decide either that you are an evolved monkey or that you are a fallen angel. This question of how you see yourself is no small matter. It radically affects how you visualize your potential. The monkey is slowly progressing up the ladder of humanity; the fallen angel can regain his full potential of divine power through a change in consciousness. One could ask how much these twin concepts of monkey and angel inform our unconscious beliefs about ourselves.

- To be, a verb giving an attribute or qualification

When we say *"this rose is red"*, the statement we make is not strictly correct because there is no red colour in nature, only varying radiations of wavelengths. The rose will appear to be red to some people but to others, the colour-blind for instance, it will appear to be green. Therefore, a more accurate statement would be *"I see this rose as red"*. This is a statement of my personal perception of reality that I do not assume is true for everyone.

- As an illustration of that, remember some argument you recently had with someone about his or your view on something.

- Try and express that disagreement using speech patterns such as: I see it as… / It is my view that…/ In my opinion…

- Then try and apply the same speech patterns in a current situation and watch the reaction of your interlocutor.

- How does using these speech patterns affect your self-esteem? How does it alter the respect you show to others?

- Expressing a (negative) opinion on someone provides us with another interesting situation. When you say "Peter is stupid" "Jane is a liar", remember that the person to whom you say this may, metaphorically speaking, see a red rose as a green rose. In other words, they may have quite a different opinion of Peter or Jane. What this means is that the defect you identify in Peter or Jane (stupidity, laziness), is not inherent in them. Peter may not be smart enough according to your standards but he may reveal smartness of a different sort in some other circumstance. The same goes for Jane: she IS not a liar, she often or occasionally chooses to lie rather than tell the truth. She might change with time.

Thinking that way offers two main advantages: it fits better with reality and it will probably improve your relationship with Peter and Jane.

The rule is: always distinguish the person and the quality or defect demonstrated by the person. Instead of talking about attributes claiming a degree of permanence let us talk about skills. A quality or defect may qualify or disqualify a person for a given management responsibility. In this particular situation, the defect only means that either he/she is not cut out for that task or he/she has to learn some skills to be able to perform it.

III - Elementalism

Elementalism refers to the mental scission or split operating in what we empirically experience as a whole.

Human beings are not composed of separate elements such as body, mind, intellect, emotions, intuition. They operate as an organism-as-a-whole-in-an-environment. If we believe in the separateness of mind and body we are led naturally to think that whatever goes on in our minds cannot affect our body and in the same way, that a healthy or an unhealthy body cannot significantly affect our mood and behaviours. But it does. Too often, we do not realize how depression or optimism can weaken or boost the immune system of both mind and body. Scientific research made on two groups of patients receiving treatment in a convalescent home showed that the group members who had found an aim and vision for their life post-illness recovered significantly faster than the group of patients who were not given the opportunity to do so. We are neither disembodied spirits floating above reality, nor solely physical bodies whose needs and constraints take over, 'imposing' on us a food-sleep-action-pleasure-pain regime. Mind and body act as a team and only by combining both together can we recreate a sense of unity in ourselves.

- The "either-or" structure.

The inappropriate use of the 'either-or' structure makes us feel we have to choose between A and B. It is the mental habit of separating and opposing two ideas, values, feelings, people: good-bad, black-white, day-night, life-death, yes-no. This 'two-value' system influ-ences our perception of ourselves as 'outside-inside our skins', thus moulding our basic conception of what is a human being.

There are no such persons as demons or angels, or to put it another way, wholly bad / wholly good people. Binary thinking is the original cause of wars and conflicts, particularly of religious or racial wars. Binary thinking results in, 'either you adopt my belief and belong to my 'family' or you oppose my beliefs so you do not belong to my family, in which case you are my enemy'.

A very different perspective adopted by Taoism considers two opposite elements not as antagonistic but as complementary states, alternating in a cyclical movement. Night becomes day, day becomes night. Yin will transition to yang. The same process applies to good and bad. Take, for example, a desirable quality like politeness: politeness turns from good to bad when it slips into hypocrisy. In time an opposite, corrective, movement is likely to emerge from that state: a renewed sense of respect leading to the reappearance of genuine good manners, and so the cycle continues, round and round. That is why a Mister Hyde can alternate with a Doctor Jekyll inside the same person.

This way of thinking brings perspective and a renewed sense of unity, of reconciliation and freedom to create and enjoy a fulfilling life.

IV - Contemplation: developing the missing element

Korzybski and scientists like Russell or Minkowski who studied the European structures of language did so in the name of science. But of course their criticisms apply equally to ordinary, every-day ways of thinking. They showed how the foundations of Aristotle's system train our minds to think restrictively about reality. Their observations and conclusions led them to suggest that what was needed was a radical shift in our thinking.

They noticed that when we think 'verbally', we project our learnt structure of language on the object of observation. By thinking 'verbally' we miss the reality and originality of that object or event. If on the contrary, we silently contemplate something, or when we 'think' without words, e.g. with images or visualizations, then we can discover new aspects or new relationships inherent in the object or event we are observing. We become able to perceive its inner structure. Then and only then does language become useful in helping us describe it as accurately as possible. Most inventors and artists use these kinds of techniques in their work.

In certain circumstances, it is helpful for all of us to distance ourselves from logical, rational discourse, in order to reconnect with our feelings, our subjectivity and our deep and meaningful experience. This is the basis for a true understanding of ourselves, our needs and motivations and it gives us greater control over our future.

The Aristotelian system breaks down external reality. It sets out to classify the world from an external standpoint. Since that does not match exactly with our inner experience – the one we live in introversion – it introduces bias into our way of relating to the world and to those around us. It creates linguistic barriers blocking our experience of ourselves as a composite, unified entity of body, mind, feelings, intelligence. Because these barriers do not fit with natural laws, they make us subservient to the opinions of external authorities which are assumed to have a better grasp of this world of logic than we have. This in turn causes us to behave as subordinates, instilling in us the feeling that 'others know better than us'. The result of this is that we are prevented from living our lives as fully as we could.

"Because ideas and words are energies which powerfully affect the physical-chemical base of our activities, Korzybski insists that "the conception of man as a mixture of animal and supernatural has for ages kept human beings captive under a deadly spell: the belief that animal selfishness and animal greediness are our essential character. The effect of this spell has been to suppress our REAL HUMAN NATURE and to prevent it from expressing itself naturally and freely".

In the following chapters, we will reconnect to the energy that circulates outside and inside ourselves, eliminating the artificial divisions created by language.

Having done this, we will consider some elements of language which can act as tools to tune into our inner world and the treasures of creativity, fulfilment and joy to be found there. Our aim will be to unify our personality, starting from the inside, to unleash our inner power and wisdom so that we can express it externally in a more genuine and accurate way.

That process will bring with it renewed optimism because, as we have already noted, optimism flourishes when we believe that we have control over our lives, when we believe that we have the capacity to change and progress and create the futures we desire. That sense of our capacity to shape our lives is what is needed for us to act and realize our goals. Great thinkers such as Abraham Maslow and Carl Gustav Jung were at pains to underline the importance of this process of self-actualization and self-realization. It is the noblest part of the human adventure on earth.

CHAPTER II

The Inner Reality: Needs and Feelings

Whenever we feel discouraged or low in spirits, when we can no longer see which path to follow, the most helpful thing we can do – in fact what we *must* do - is to turn our gaze inward to focus on our inner world which is where each of us lives the most intimate part of our lives. Friends and relations can offer all sorts of advice on what we should or should not do but only I can decide for myself how to live my life. And I will make better decisions about that if I have a good grasp of how my inner world functions.

I - Getting in touch with one's needs

If we are happy we welcome new experiences, relationships and projects. Happiness gives us access to our natural creativity. Studies have shown that feeling happy about life and making plans for the future have the additional benefit of making us more careful about eating healthily, abler to foster healthy and positive relations with others, and more likely to discover new talents in ourselves. This reservoir of positive feelings also enables us deal more effectively with any difficulties we encounter. Anxiety on the other hand, tends to lock us into unhelpful, repetitive patterns, while fear can stop us acting altogether.

Unpleasant feelings like anxiety, fear, sadness induce reactions in us which match the threats we perceive. Fear may make us act to avoid a danger but it may also keep us literally rooted to the spot. Anger makes us say what we do or do not want, especially in cases involving our physical or emotional security. But anger endangers our relationships and is not in itself a constructive response. These kinds of feelings all belong in the category labelled 'survival'. They tend to perpetuate the same thought processes and the same automatic responses, blocking off new ways of thinking.

- Unmet needs give rise to emotional turbulence

We have to listen to our feelings. Our understanding of the world is conditioned by two dominant factors: language and culture, but there is one other we must take account of, namely our own personal experiences which form the basis on which we make judgements about what is or is not good for us. This is what is often called our 'Weltanschauung' or our view of the world. We generally experience a painful emotional reaction when an event triggers a warning of danger or discomfort.

Since we constantly seek to protect our inner stability each time we experience such a negative feeling the principle of homeostasis, (i.e. the effort the psychic body makes to maintain a stable equilibrium), will trigger the classic responses of flight, aggression or passive acceptance.

The equilibrium we aspire to can be found however by another route if we can make sense of what is happening to us in other terms. Even the most unfavourable circumstances – a failure of some kind or a loss for example - can be beneficial if they lead us towards new achievements. That is what Tom Sawyer, Mark Twain's mischievous hero, discovers when he is told his punishment will be to repaint the fence round his parents' house. His friends stand jeering at him outside the house but Tom is determined not to lose face. What does he do? He tells them that he is doing this task as a favour, 'for a lark'. He turns the job into a creative exercise so that, one by one, his friends beg to be allowed to contribute to this great work. The result is that before the day has even drawn to a close the fence is repainted, Tom has escaped the worst of his punishment and in the process has enhanced his prestige with his friends.

We can adopt another tactic. We can decide to give up trying to protect ourselves from the situation as it is presented to us and focus instead on what is really happening inside us. Whichever tactic we adopt the aim is the same: to free up the positive energy flowing in each one of us, to release what keeps us happy and healthy. That feeling of being fully alive, spontaneous and joyful is something we typically experience when we are on holiday and we can follow our desires and creative ideas in a more relaxed and joyful atmosphere.

- Widening the scope of our thinking

If we cling to the habit of projecting onto the future our fears of loss and suffering we are bound to keep revisiting the same worn-out, poor-quality thoughts.

And the more we allow ourselves to do this, the more engrained these habits of negativity become. The result of this is that it becomes harder and harder to visualize oneself as a creative being.

 In this respect the structure of Western languages is the opposite of helpful. As we saw in chapter 1, European languages place great emphasis on the 'identity principle'. Not only does the verb 'to be' introduce confusion between the subject and its attribute – for example, the statement, 'I'm an idiot' would be much more accurate if it were rephrased and said, 'I did something stupid' instead – the verb also suggests that everyone is a separate individual, utterly distinct from any other. If you take a look at Chinese on the other hand, you see that it places much more stress on the relationships and interactions between people and things. Other Oriental languages do likewise. The difference is dramatic. It means that we in the West see ourselves as separate, autonomous individuals. The problem is that that autonomy does not just bring with it a sense of our individual aloneness, we also lose the awareness of the wider context in which we live and onto which we project our future plans. The result of this is either that we end up burdened more than we need to be or that we act as if what we do is our business and nobody else's.

- Discerning and choosing

What is our inner world made of? Of ideas, feelings, spiritual states or states of being.

When we modify our perceptions we also modify our experiences which in turn modify our state of mind. Our state of mind is critical in affecting the quality of the interactions we have with our physical and relational environment.

Gregory Bateson is both an ethnologist and a psychologist, and his theoretical work on communication has been a major source of inspiration for the founders of NLP (Neuro-Linguistic Programming). He has analysed the links between mental illness and the environment and in his book, 'Towards an ecology of the mind', Bateson describes the mind as a system composed of both the subject and his/her environment. He emphasizes that the mind, which according to his theory includes ideas, thoughts, and feelings, is permeable to external influences. His analysis leads him to suggest that one of the ways to maintain good mental health is by eliminating from one's own environment the toxic elements in one's relations or one's ideas. This assumes the individual has available to him/her a fluidity or plasticity which enables him or her to manage those external influences without allowing them to affect him/her in a negative way.

The problem is that we tend to be quite attached to the ideas and people we know best. We like what we know. It makes us feel safe and it saves us having to think. Feeling safe is a basic human need. Every child needs a minimum of security to grow up in conditions of harmony and wellbeing. Nevertheless, security does not necessarily mean nothing changes. The fact is that change is one of the defining characteristics of life on earth. To quote Heraclitus, « *The only permanent and constant feature of life is change* ».

The stability which makes us feel secure comes when there is no turbulence in our inner world, because such turbulence is always felt as disagreeable. Fluctuations occur when one is optimistic one day, but sad or depressed the next. If one starts out full of enthusiasm for a project but quickly develops doubts and uncertainties regarding it, the strength inherent in the initial concept is lost. Of course it is possible to rekindle the early flame. However, there is still a risk that the inner balance of the spirit, what we can call its ecology, has been disturbed so that its natural growth has been compromised.

II - Needs and feelings

- Our three primary needs

Our three basic needs correspond to the hierarchy of needs which are present in the development of the individual from infancy through to adulthood, as formulated by Abraham Maslow. Those needs must be met first of all because it is by satisfying them that the adult can go on to pursue other, higher goals. They are:

Feeling safe and secure. We need to be able to eat, drink and sleep without feeling threatened. We need to feel the peace that results from that sense of physical security so that we can go forward confidently in our lives.

Being loved and accepted in our family or community. We also need to both receive and give love by showing affection, consideration and compassion for others.

Acquiring a sense of self-worth. We need to feel secure in our sense of self-worth by being recognized for what we are. But we must also accept and appreciate who we are ourselves, and we must cultivate our talents. That means rekindling our inner flame, opening ourselves up to life, cultivating a sense of curiosity for the new discoveries life offers, whether those discoveries are new friendships, new ideas, or the thousand and one other adventures awaiting us, including of course, the adventure of discovering who one really is.

Meeting these three needs is a prerequisite for satisfying our wider desires for fulfilment and **happiness**.

If we have the good fortune to be born into a loving and protective family and if we show, we have skills and talents which those around us recognize there will be no problem about meeting them. Even if this is not the case, there are other ways of meeting those needs.

- The ultimate need to grow and evolve

The whole process of evolution, from the purely physical to the spiritual, takes place through this process of satisfying the primary needs. We all need to belong to a human community of some kind, and we all want to develop our talents. Those two needs are fundamental to the socialized human being. However, if we become too comfortable with our lives there is a risk we become rigidified, we develop the negative side of the skills we have acquired. Boredom, or alternatively egoism, a wish to control or dominate, often lies at the root of conflicts and discontent in each of us and in those around us.

It is for that reason that we occasionally have to heed what our life is trying to tell us and we have to let a different image of ourselves and our role emerge. As an example of this, think of how once parents become grandparents they substitute patience and loving kindness for the controlling role they previously performed.

As we go through life we need to acquire **wisdom** to help us discover what is truly right for us, recognizing that we must not accept unquestioningly what we have absorbed through culture, education and received opinion. Wisdom is what will help us overcome our problems and find new sources of inspiration.

What at this point in your life are the things that motivate you? What are your hopes and aspirations?

Ask yourself these questions:

- What is my deepest need or desire at this moment in terms of being (not of having?)

- Who or what do I want to become?

- What interests me, motivates me and nurtures my psychological wellbeing?

- What would motive me to take action, to do whatever is necessary to reach my goal?

- Ecology or one's self-image in one's environment

To come back to the concept of ecology, the science which studies living beings and their interactions with their surroundings, perhaps we have not realized the extent to which the dualism so dominant in Western culture has prevented us from appreciating the interplay between the mind and the body, between the body, the mind and the environment. And because we have not appreciated the importance of this we have deprived ourselves of our innate capacity to master our spiritual and emotional states.

We persist in neglecting our spiritual wellbeing. The effect is the same as when we fail to give a plant the warmth and water it needs to grow: it withers and droops. The truth bears repeating: **body and mind are intimately linked**. More and more doctors are convinced that patients who constantly entertain negative thoughts and feelings are liable to experience a loss of mental and physical energy which, in the longer term, may well result in health problems. This means that understanding our needs and feelings, especially those relating to our physical and mental wellbeing, is essential if we wish to take our place happily in the human community, express our innate qualities and our individual talents.

But we are much more than merely physical beings. Our deepest needs are those which we have as spiritual beings. Studies in positive psychology show that demonstrating positive feelings such as gratitude, kindness and compassion, does indeed nourish the spirituality in each of us. To use a gardening analogy again, we know that plants grow because they have the right conditions for that growth, not because someone tells them to!

You have reached a certain point in your life. Now ask yourself these questions:

- What do I need to rethink in my life?

- What part of me is begging to be heard and developed? For instance, should I listen more to what my heart is telling me, what my feminine side longs for? Would it be better for

me if I was less focused on the « masculine » qualities of precision and productivity?

- Do I pay enough attention to my need for rest when I am tired, or to my need for nature, clean air and healthy food?

- Is it time for me to become a mentor, so that I can transmit what I know to others?

- Should I take better care of my environment and be more proactive in protecting this planet I live on?

- Do I think big enough? Do I cultivate an image of myself as someone who is strong and positive?

If we begin to address these questions we will find that, no matter what is going on around us, we will stop blaming fate and bad luck, we will not allow ourselves to sink into despair. We can use this ecological approach instead, knowing that it will both restore and nourish the wellbeing of our system. By system what is meant is each one of us in interaction with our environment, our personal relations, the natural world and where we live. The site of that interaction is first and foremost to be found within our minds. If we can maintain our system in harmonious equilibrium, we will be rewarded with happiness rather than suffering the pains of loss and disappointment.

III - So what shall we do?

It is generally the case that people become less optimistic when they start thinking about the challenges facing them, for example:

- What is happening in the wider world and in their own immediate environment;

- Their feeling of not being strong or skilled enough to deal with what they see, whether it is in choosing what to do, how to behave or in having the necessary skills.

The solution to these anxieties is to be found on a different plane from the problem itself. It lies in working with the beliefs and values that best fit the stage we have each reached in our own development. The freedom the adolescent demands reflects the need of the adolescent to assert his or her individuality. With the onset of the adult years and an increasing awareness of the laws of action and reaction, that demand for freedom becomes more nuanced. Freedom we learn, stops where the freedom of others comes into play. **True freedom lies less in action and more in our capacity to remain happy if we decide to do so.**

- Dealing with perceptions and emotions

There is a direct link between our perceptions and our emotions. Our nervous system sets up correlations between what we perceive as reality and the interpretations we make of what we perceive. Those correlations may be either useful or harmful. If you are the victim of an attack at night you are very likely to experience the same feelings each time you find yourself in circumstances which activate the memory of that attack, even if there is objectively no real danger. All that is needed is the outline of a presumed aggressor, darkness and solitude for you to be seized with panic.

The emotion may engulf you with all its violence (e.g. panic, terror), or remain buried beneath the layers of the unconscious, showing itself for example in procrastination, putting off doing something you know you ought to do because of the negative associations it has. In either case there are three ways of tackling the problem:

1. Accept the feelings. First acknowledge which situations trigger feelings of unease, anxiety, anger, resentment. If it is impossible to change those situations one solution is to look at what is going on inside, you honestly and non-judgementally. This means identifying with the feeling, accepting what it is telling you, allowing the strong sensations it generates in you to flow through your body as well as your mind. By practising this concentrated attention, the feeling will diminish in due course and eventually disappear altogether.

2. Alternately you may take on the role of the observer. This requires you to take a non-judgemental stance – no taking sides, no expectations – so that you can see more clearly what is really going on in the dilemma or difficulty facing you. To borrow from quantum physics, we can say that the problem behaves like the particle. It transforms into a wave and the wave moves, changing shape as it does so.

As Gregory Bateson said, the observer, the object observed and the process of observation form a whole. The observer chooses and constructs his individual reality but what is more surprising is that he then treats this constructed reality as if it has a verifiably independent existence!

A useful technique consists in detaching oneself mentally from the situation you are involved in. This allows you to have an overarching view of what is going on with the other participants as if you were watching yourself and them from a distance or from above. The nature and quality of each of the protagonists and the feelings they have become clearer. Your perceptions are changed by what you observe. You have a better understanding of the issues so you can begin to see the outline of a possible solution.

3. Deliberately altering our perceptions. We often forget that change is constant. The world runs on change even if that change is sometimes so slow it is imperceptible to the human consciousness. But a time may come when we realise that we are no longer in harmony with certain aspects of our lives. We may decide to change how we live or how we adapt to circumstances. But there may also come a time when we find we need to go even further, to re-examine how we see both the world outside and in our inner reality.

The best way to do this is go back to the bedrock: to observe and challenge our thought patterns, and to change how we express ourselves. That will be the subject of the next chapter.

CHAPTER III

The Invocational Power of Words – a Creative act

Our feelings of dissatisfaction, fears, desires, optimism and pessimism all leave an imprint of energy. Just as radio waves, and others invisible to the human eye impact on the environment so do thoughts and feelings. Our thoughts and feelings have their own frequency. Whatever we say or think leaves an imprint.

A positive, optimistic thought can do far more to change our reality than one that focuses on our dissatisfactions or our disappointments.

I - Formulating our wishes clearly – the first step towards making them a reality

Simply saying « I've had enough of this » is not the answer. All it does is fix the dissatisfaction even more firmly inside me. Likewise, « *I must give up smoking. I must cut down on sugar* » is just as unhelpful.

The mind is very literal. It doesn't distinguish between negation and affirmation. Those instructions **not** to do or be etc. something actually produce the opposite of the intended effect. If someone tells you not to think about a pink elephant, what happens is that you immediately start to think of an elephant. Your mind then begins to add the colour pink to that elephant and in no time at all it is completely absorbed in thinking of exactly what it was instructed not to do.

In the same way, if we are faced with a problem which we cannot resolve by logic it is better to give up thinking about it. If we go on letting our thoughts dwell on it, we are doing the same thing as when we keep focusing on the pink elephant we have been asked not to think about. We are going round and round in circles, rehashing the same unprofitable thoughts with no useful outcome.

A better way to proceed is to ask ourselves what we want. We have all sorts of desires. Some of them, whether they spring from the lure of consumerism or from our desire to be like this or that celebrity, drain us of our energy, because they alienate us from who we really are, from our inner truth. There are others however, which are much closer to the real reasons for our being here on earth.

Let us think for a moment about the etymology of the word 'desire'. It comes from the Latin *sidus, sideris*: constellation, star. The word was used by sailors when they could find no star in the sky by which to guide their vessel. If we understand the meaning of 'desire' in this way, we see that the word expresses more than simply a lack. It is a signal, a powerful impulse which urges us towards what we pine for: heaven, a blessed state.

Let us try to give a concrete expression to this desire. Ask yourself these questions:

- Is there a void in your life?

- What are your dreams?

- What kind of life do you truly want to live?

- What might it be like? Can you be precise?

- If you could make it real what would you feel?

It is important to be pragmatic about this - there is no point crying for the moon. For instance, try to imagine what a harmonious relationship with someone central to your life would be like. What attitude, behaviour or atmosphere would you expect to find? How would you talk to one another? What else might be different?

Be as precise as you can:

- "I would like to be happy". Is that precise enough? What makes you happy (or could make you happy)? What do you really need? A job that you enjoy? What kind of job? What kind of salary do you want from it? How much autonomy do you want? How much responsibility?

The way to tackle the question is by breaking the desired reality down into its component parts. These can then become primary and secondary objectives to be aimed for. It may become apparent for example, that you need some kind of further training or education if your desired goal is to be given more responsibility.

If our goals really motivate us they will carry us forward on a current of energy and there is much less likelihood of us falling into a state of hope-less-ness.

- The power of words

In some ancient languages words have an inherent power which finds expression in mantras. In modern languages we tend not to experience the direct vibrationary effect of words on our minds.

It is worth remembering however, that the word 'mantra' is made up of the root *man* meaning to think and the suffix *'-tra'*, which means tool or instrument. A mantra is a verbal tool which acts on the mind. It can also be described as a means of channelling the mind's tendency to roam and it can serve as a tool for protection, prayer or celebration.

Furthermore, a mantra acts like a kind of mental training programme and it does this because the repetition of it has an impact on our brains. When we make use of the positivity and strength in our imaginations we become able to achieve both our personal and our professional goals, but even more importantly, to give full expression to our talents, our initiative and our responsibility. This is reason enough to feel optimistic!

Émile Coué, the French psychologist and pharmacist, developed a not dissimilar method which has since become world-famous. In summary the *Coué* Method acts like a kind of self-fulfilling prophecy and is based on suggestion and self-hypnosis.

Emile *Coué's* favourite mantra was, « Every day, in every way, I am getting better and better ». The trick, he said, was to repeat it several times over every day. Does that sound naive or silly? Let's think about it. If when we were teenagers we were constantly being told, « You're useless, you're not good at anything, you'll never do anything with your life», it is quite possible that we have ended up believing exactly that. In that case why would a statement that says the opposite not act as powerfully upon us as did those negative judgements?

If you know exactly what you want to change one very straightforward way is therefore to make yourself a mantra, a positive statement about the change you wish to make and say that to yourself several times a day until you see a change in yourself. For example, if you are often impatient with your children say to yourself « I am patient. There are hidden depths of patience in me ». Repeat that several times every day for three weeks and see how it changes your behaviour.

II - Creative words

As the philosopher, Henri Bergson, pointed out, science and its concepts use a generalising approach to knowledge: they focus on the common features of things which are in other respects quite different. What Bergson was looking for were ways of seeing and hearing which would take account of the **uniqueness** of things. That is also our aim here.

As we have already noted, what we believe is an objective reality is in fact a creation of the mind. The reality we perceive comes from the perceptions we have of the external world via our sense organs, our beliefs and our life experiences.

« *Words are not things. The map is not the territory* » as Alfred Korzybski said. The analogy of the map is a useful one here: a map shows the roads, mountains and forests. We use it to guide us into that territory, the plains and mountains, the dense, dark forests. Indirectly, the map also gives us access to more than just landscape: to the scents and textures - the cut hay, the hard, sharp stones under our feet - and to the emotions generated: joy and awe at the beauty of the landscape.

Just as a map will guide us through a physical space, words can be powerful guides to our inner feelings. This is especially true of abstract words. Because they are abstract they can carry a whole host of both objective and subjective meanings. They only have to 'speak to us' to open us up to new meanings and understandings.

Words have the power to conjure up a reality. When we name something we make it exist, i.e. we bring a new reality alive. Let us be clear that what comes first, before experience itself or the identification of that experience, is the experimenter him or herself, alert, aware, watchful. We are each of us observers in that sense.

This means that nothing stands in the way of our immersing ourselves in a word, so as to draw from it some new, deeper meaning. That process of immersion gives us a further way of distancing ourselves from the taken-for-granted ideas and concepts which are so common in our society. Immersing ourselves in a word allows us to break through the barriers and frontiers of language. When we find the vital core of a word like peace or love, it takes on a new life inside us.

One other method is to draw out the essence of the words we use by putting them through what we might call the filter of silence and meditation. Once we reach this step in this restructuring of our reality or our life plan we can start using grammar in a completely new way:

- The noun or the power of naming

When I name something I make it exist. That is an extraordinary statement. It means that we are endowed with an almost godlike power over our external reality!

It is preferable to use a 'right brain' approach with some abstract nouns, particularly those which touch us most intimately. The right brain is the non-analytic, non-reasoning side of the brain which questions less and tends on the whole to give us a global and positive view of things.

Abstract words have a particular quality, namely that they can take on a range of different meanings. The word 'freedom' can mean a dozen different things, depending on your perspective: more freedom to do as you please even if what you want to do will inconvenience your neighbour, or the right to think as you wish without feeling you are constrained by outside authorities and influences.

Words have also an evocative power as the poetic arts show so well. The sea and the sky are both much more than an expanse of water or an overarching dome of ever-changing colour. They have a symbolic dimension; they conjure up memories which feed our souls. They bring us right into our inner world.

If we think about the word 'desire' again for a moment, the verb *desiderare*, in Latin means to note the absence of something, in the case of desire it originally meant the absence of stars in the sailors' night sky.

Considerare, another Latin verb, means the exact opposite: to note the presence of something, and by extension 'to consider' it, to examine it, or we might say, to look more closely at the stars in this world I am creating.

Meditation consists of holding an object of contemplation or reflexion in your mind long enough for the meaning of it to emerge from the word which describes it. What is revealed in that process will be a meaning which is yours alone or - even more exciting - a meaning which, transcending individual understanding, touches the universal. Words are not empty vessels. It is up to us to find what they really hold.

If what matters to you is truth or justice, hold that word in your mind. Allow it to disperse its particular 'scent' inside you. Be patient, wait and let it reveal itself so that it brings you to a sense of peace, order and stillness. This is not about exercising your powers of reasoning or philosophising intellectually about the meaning of the word in question. The aim is to strip away those ways of experiencing and perceive the essence of the word directly.

If the word 'autonomy' is important to you in the kind of job you would like to do, think very carefully about what this word means to you, what it contains. Is it the absence of constraints? Of course it must partly be that, but what else is it? What particular 'star' shines out of that word: independence, self-realisation, fulfilments, breaking free of your self-imposed limitations? Try to be as precise as possible about the exact meaning it has for you.

While exploring the potential of whichever word you are contemplating, it helps to try and visualize it as well, to feel what emotions it evokes in you. Doing this will make your discovery of its depths and true meaning even stronger and firmer.

- Adjectives - the wonder of description

The adjective's role is to make a word more precise, to give it colour and character.

We should use adjectives knowingly. « *I am ….* ». We can put in inverted commas those qualities we would like to have or acquire. « *I am worthy of love or respect* ». « *I am capable of doing this job* » And in saying or thinking this, feel what it is saying to you. Capable! What does that adjective make you feel? Listen to your feelings. Any anger inside you will dissipate and you will know who you truly are.

- Verbs - acting, making things happen

I stop thinking or reflecting and I act.

If you decide you want to take control of your future it follows naturally that some kind of action, however big or small, will be required. The best approach in that case is to use verbs in the present tense or in the near future and to make sure you frame positive sentences.

What is the first thing I must do if I wish to become autonomous? That film I was told was worth seeing - perhaps, instead of waiting and hoping that someone will go with me to see it, I ought to go and see by myself? Doing things in small steps is a very good way of proceeding. It stops you feeling the challenge is too great and that it requires more energy than you can summon.

- The power of positive thoughts

If you find yourself constantly rehearsing negative thoughts, try turning the system on its head and make yourself think a good thought instead in a conscious and deliberate way. It is said that for every negative thought you need at a minimum one positive thought and furthermore that positive thought must have a strong positive weighting to combat the negativity.

Thought precedes action. But if we only think and don't also act not much will happen. That kind of thinking is no better than day-dreaming. However, a thought which evokes a feeling or an emotion can have a transformative effect. We must choose a thought that we believe in, one which either lifts our spirits or fills us with joy and which in so doing enhances our sense of self-worth. But choosing such a thought is not like leafing through a catalogue and picking something out at random.

« *I don't know how to do this. But I do know how to do that and that's what I will do.* » When I do it that is my first step on the way to the life I want to live.

Pay attention to words like 'to try' and 'perhaps' and all the other words that convey indecision and uncertainty about whether you can succeed in what you want to achieve.

When everything is going badly find some positive act to do which will lift you out of your feeling of hope-less-ness and give you a more optimistic view of the future.

Supposing you have low self-esteem, saying « *I am a good person* » may not be enough to convince you of that. It is more effective to think something like, « *I accept me as I am and I appreciate myself for who I am.* » You can then add to that by saying something like, « *I am confident about life and my life shows me I am right to be so.* »

- Adverbs - intensifying an action

Some adverbs must be used with circumspection, e.g. « *never* », « *always* ». Events and people change. We should not dismiss the possibility of an improvement in something or someone even before it happens. The best is to avoid all phrases like « *I'll never manage it* », « *I'm always last* »

Think of examples of times when you successfully did something difficult or when you came first at something. Better still find a way of rephrasing in a more nuanced way the criticism you made of yourself: « *It's proving quite difficult for me to do that… at present* ». « *I'm always last… in maths… this year* ».

Avoid words and phrases like « *very* », « *too much* », « *too late* ». Is it ever too late to do something well?

There is another technique for shaking off a bad mood. Take the case of a mother who says to her child, « *I'm very cross with you* ». She may not really mean it as strongly as it sounds but she wants to be quite sure her child knows she is not pleased. That desire is understandable but it would be preferable if instead of using the 'very' she could say quite simply, « *I am cross with you* ». In almost all cases that statement is all that is needed for the child to understand.

The statement can be reinforced by using an affirmation which draws on Loving Communication: *« I am not happy when you (don't tidy your room, when you do or don't do this or that) ».* By putting it like this the criticism becomes precise and practical both for the listener and the speaker. The emotion is removed from the situation and the likelihood of conflict is much less. The child is not left feeling he is 'useless'. He knows that all that is being asked of him is that he tidies his room. And, to add even more to the positivity the child might be told something like, *« And I would like you to help me make the sandwiches for your birthday party as well. »* At which point the idea of tidying his room suddenly becomes an altogether more enjoyable prospect.

- Words and the brain

Neuroscience has taught us that we do not come fully formed into this world when we are born. What is called 'neural plasticity' is that capacity of the brain to create new neural circuits each time we learn new skills. But that is not all. As well as this capacity to acquire new skills the brain can make us more flexible and more optimistic. That is because every time we feel optimistic we either create or we strengthen certain neural connections in our brains (synapses). It is that neural activity which makes us more optimistic and enthusiastic, and it happens inside us in the most natural way.

CHAPTER IV

The Invisible Reality – An Ocean of Goodness

If it is possible for us to open our understanding of the world to a new reality beyond words, what is this reality which is hidden behind that facade?

I - The invisible reality or the soul of being

Feelings are our main source of energy. They are what drive us and what give us our life force. We do not live to talk. We live to communicate with others and our communication, our exchanges are what make us feel alive. Likewise, we do not live to think, we live to use our judgement, our creativity. Nor do we live to act. We act in order to know we are alive.

Everything we do we do in order to feel ourselves fully alive, active and engaged with our fellow men. That means drawing on the whole spectrum of needs, feelings and emotions we looked at in Chapter 2. Together they function like an engine inside us, although we are not always aware of that; we hear words, we see gestures without always paying enough attention to the intentions and feelings behind them.

Similarly, we are not always aware of our own feelings, even though those feelings may be quite apparent from our facial expressions or the way we hold ourselves. Our psychic energy is working while we are speaking or acting.

Before materialism became the dominant paradigm, what we used to call soul or spirit was understood as the vibrating invisible reality which surrounds us, is in us and is our life-source. We can open ourselves to those vibrations, make contact with this ocean of qualities any time we wish.

The world of art gives us a good illustration of this:

A dancer's body, the physical structure of bones, muscle and tendons, is the living instrument the choreographer uses for his creation. You have to be part of a dance class, or watching from the side-lines, to understand what is being asked of the dancer. « *Can I have more lightness in that leap, more fullness in that jump, more elevation in that pirouette?* » says the teacher. And the pupil whose muscles already know the movement, has to search in his or her soul for the extra which is being asked of him or her. In other words, the spirit of the dance is only partly to be found in the correct execution of a set of movements. What matters much more is how the dancer uses his/her body as an instrument to express the idea, feeling, intention within those movements. The spirit of the dance is born in the soul of the dancer.

When we manage to connect with our creative energy, whether we do this through art, or by meditating on the full meaning of a word, or by some immediate experience of the natural world, what happens is a letting-go, a feeling of calm and of one's mind opening up. We have touched a reality which feels deep and true. Even if later we catch ourselves falling back on old habits, talking negatively again or expressing doubts such as, « *I am incapable of...* » that interior dialogue has much less hold on us because we know we have lived a different kind of experience, one of the beauty and goodness inside each of us which we feel when we are truly ourselves.

The deeper the experience, the deeper the imprint made in our brains and the easier it is to retrace that imprint. Think of it like the marks of your footsteps across a meadow. Tomorrow you will see where you walked by the track you made through the grass and if you take this path every day you will see it more and more clearly. Neuroscience has played an important role in helping us understand that our personalities are by no means fixed by the time we reach the end of our teenage years. We now know that we go on changing indefinitely, either by learning new skills or by new experiences. Thus it is that neuroscience has given us a further reason for overcoming that temporary loss of confidence in ourselves, since every effort we make is rewarded by an imprint on our brains and in our memory bank.

- What to do when we feel 'blocked'

Nevertheless, not everything starts in the brain. The brain behaves rather like a pivot revolving between our psychic energy and the outward expression of that energy. Loosening the feeling of being stuck either in relation to an activity we are engaged in or in how our mind is working has to be done in stages:

- As we saw in Chapter 2 if we feel blocked it is always useful to go back and ask ourselves again how we want to live and what creative energy we can call on.

- If we feel there is resistance or there are obstacles in the way or if our body itself indicates that there is a blockage, what we must do is shed more light on the situation. The body is not just a mechanism. It functions in partnership with the mind in all its various different states. It is our primary vehicle of communication with the world and other people. It is also the seat of feelings and emotions which themselves inform us about our mental state. We need to pay attention and respond to the signals the body sends out: how it is reacting, whether it is upset, disturbed etc. Noticing our heightened emotion which we can perhaps feel through the tightening of the muscles in our throat or the knot in our stomach, and staying with that emotion allows the virulence of it to dissipate as we gain a better understanding of where that feeling originates. If strong feelings are triggered at the thought of a situation we want very badly to prevent or avoid or a task which we feel is impossible, then both the emotion and the memory associated with it which between them are provoking this reaction,

must be fully experienced so that they can be absorbed and integrated.

- Once this process is complete – i.e. both the emotion and its trigger have been accepted and processed – we can proceed. We are going to seek out resources on different levels. These will enable us to act without reacting and construct whatever it is we want. The answer may lie inside us – perhaps we need to readjust our expectations, rethink our attitude or the behaviour which has triggered the negative feeling. Or perhaps we can look for an answer in our immediate environment: maybe to consult other people, or take inspiration from them. Or perhaps take a trip into the countryside, move house, learn new skills. There are hundreds if not thousands of ways by which we can gain more insight into ourselves and our situation and release the blockage that has been holding us back.

- If we are receptive we can seize fleeting opportunities which come our way. By paying attention to the context, i.e. to those who make approaches to us, to relationships and other connections we become able to draw inspiration from a huge, ever-changing pool of resources.

II - The force field of consciousness

Nowadays, scientists agree that energy fields of one sort and another – gravitational, electromagnetic, quantum to name but some of them - make up the basic structure of the physical universe. Energy exists in different forms and all those forms are grouped into 'fields'. Nature may appear to us as a solid mass but that is only how we perceive it with our sense organs. The fields of invisible energy which structure and animate the universe are the organising principles on which the whole is founded. They form the linkages between living beings and things. Energy manifests itself in a range of different ways, through light, heat, chemical reactions etc.

What we can call the force field of consciousness is an infinite reserve of vibrating energy, supple enough to make it possible for us to be in tears one moment and laughing out loud the next. The energy contained in our feelings expresses itself both mentally in our 'psychic field' and externally in the various activities we engage in and our relationships with others. We all know that it is not the hammer which drives the nail home, it is the hand that holds it and the hand that holds it is actioned by the intention behind it - the energy of the thought and the determination to hang a picture on the wall, for instance, or mend a piece of furniture.

Our mental fields are definitely affected by the milieu we live in and by our antecedents. But our thoughts and feelings and our sense of self are what generate the energy that revitalizes that internal reality. At any moment we can feel devoid of the energy required for a task but equally we can resist the lure of self-doubt, denial, and fear, all of which the intellect readily puts before us, and retrieve a sense of coherence, unity and inner well-being. The trick is to master the controlling, divisive ego which is constantly urging us to look outwards to find security, pleasure or power. Surpassing the narrow filter of the ego which limits one's field of vision, means gaining access to a greatly enlarged field of perceptions and a whole host of other information.

That is the state which one can attain through meditation. It is a state of mind which can be reached for example, by watching a beautiful sunset or listening to a Mozart sonata, and it is almost certainly the state of mind of creative artists of every kind. Mozart said that he didn't create the music he wrote. The music came to him, which is another way of describing what we usually call inspiration. Both art and nature provide us with the type of inspiration which help us to become fully ourselves, effortlessly, just by being in harmony with the beauty there in front of us, filling our mind and body with peace and tranquillity. If we allow ourselves to become fully absorbed in it, we begin to feel other subtler feelings, we experience the balm of being at one with ourselves and nature. We enter a realm of limitless beauty and joy.

III - The 'particles' of belief

Quantum physics has enabled us to extend our understanding beyond the concept of visible particles to an underlying entity: energy fields invisible to the human eye.

The mechanistic theory of the atom as a fixed and permanent element in space has given way to the idea of the atom as a structure of activity within those energy fields. Physicists have proved that sub-atomic particles can be both particles and waves.

As an example of this we know that light acts simultaneously as a wave and as a particle (photons are the elementary particles of which light waves are composed). Furthermore, quantum mechanics has shown that the observer of this phenomenon affects that wave-particle duality. In the most basic way therefore, we can say that the observer plays a creative role in the process. Once we know that there is this flux of state at the deepest, most fundamental level of our universe we can let go of our determinist view of matter as a fixed, immutable entity and consequently of the feeling of impotence such a view engenders. Instead we can proceed knowing that we are the creators of our own reality.

The mirroring effect can play its part in everyday life. Not that we mean to change people into waves but that we can help them change their attitude! For example, if a grown-up sees a child about to do something silly and the child herself knows she is being observed, the child will in all probability not do whatever it is she was planning to do. She will gravitate to some other act which she knows will be more acceptable to the watching adult.

We have all had the experience of being the creative observer. The teacher watching a group of children can see the way in which the energy of the group circulates within it through the medium of constantly evolving interactions. She sees shyness and fear in one corner, aggression and assertiveness in another and round about the swirling movement of the majority of the group, waiting in a state of uncommitted availability. Everything is there in that group. Which will she choose to foster?

The same approach can be used with our psychic field and the forms our thoughts and beliefs take. We tend to visualise them as solid particles but they can actually change shape and take new configurations if we examine them closely. They can resolve in unexpected ways and lose the solidity we attribute to them.

Our beliefs are thought patterns which we have acquired through our upbringing and our previous experiences. They tend to set arbitrary limits on us and their concern is usually to do with what we are or are not allowed to think about ourselves in relation either to our potential success, or the person we really are. *« Money is dirty. » « We don't do that kind of thing in our family. » « You don't have the right to succeed. » « That's life. Get on with it. »*

Thinking of our mind energy field like this we can see that there are broadly two options if for example, we have a setback at work: we can either get stuck on a 'thought particle' or send out a 'thought wave', a more flexible, fluid way of envisaging the situation. The thought forms *« I am a good person »*, *« I have every right to success »* have the merit of drawing energy in towards attainable objectives.

If we think of ourselves as a good manager, a gifted student, a loyal friend, those beliefs will help preserve a positive frame of mind and in due course influence the results we see from our efforts.

Whatever we think about ourselves doesn't stay locked away in a corner of our minds. It impacts directly on the results we achieve and how we tackle our challenges whether the challenge is to put up a shelf or revise for an exam.

IV - Representing the future

Quantum theory demonstrates that when something comes into being in the material world what precedes that physical manifestation is a pulse of energy. The pulse of energy may originate in an intention, a feeling, an actual plan, which that invisible vital force of creative energy takes hold of and transforms. Since this is the case we know that our thoughts, feelings and beliefs have a creative and proactive power which we cannot afford to ignore.

Once we accept that our reality is directly affected by our energy state we can stop seeing the external world, other people, or even ourselves as to blame for what is not working in our lives. We realise what is needed instead, is to take a good look at our emotional and mental energy levels. The corollary of this is that we must strive to behave in ways which are in harmony with our intentions and desires because we also know that our behaviour itself generates a vibratory energy which is communicated to those round about us. Supposing I want to be on better terms with my colleagues, what I should start by doing is ensuring that I behave with consideration and courtesy towards them. A small but relevant example would be for instance, instead of just opening a window near where my colleague has his desk, asking him first if he minds if I do. A little thing like that can reap much more than its own rewards in terms of improving the atmosphere of the office!

In the longer term tactics like that to help us achieve the result we want are far more effective in every way than enforcing one's will in a high-handed fashion. High-handedness will get you a result in the short term but will prove counter-productive over time. Of course one can get cooperation by force or coercion, just as one can use it to get other changes in behaviour or a rise in productivity. But the risks attendant on that way of proceeding are immense: they are likely to generate resistance which then sets up other tensions, leading to a progressive deterioration in relations between those concerned.

Our internal dialogue is often at work, weaving the pattern of our future, not always in the most optimistic terms. « *I am no good at languages* » may well be an undeniable truth in the present moment but it is not much help in showing me how to change that. If the aim, is to achieve something concrete in your life, it is far more useful to study or work towards that aim, or to focus on subjects and activities which you know you can do successfully. If we can visualise a positive outcome for whatever we wish to do and we assert this strongly to ourselves, the outcome will almost certainly meet our expectations and hopes much more closely than if we start out with doubts and uncertainties. « *I mustn't mess this up...* » is not a helpful way to begin anything.

It is not so much a question of elaborating strategic plans three months or three years in advance but much more to do with periodically checking in on our inner dialogue, seeing how we are talking to ourselves both individually and collectively about our aims, our future, our skills and our strengths. The sociologist Fred Pollack carried out a study in the 1970s on the rise and fall of cultures and his work showed convincingly that one of the key reasons for the disappearance of cultures was when the society in question no longer held an image of its future. It is therefore crucial to keep the future in mind, to dream up projects, to hold onto visions which are both realistic in terms of one's current reality but which are also the vectors of change and hope.

This attitude of realism coupled with inspiration is rooted in our ability to use our strengths and our knowledge to the utmost. What good practices and what particular strengths do we need to nurture and develop in the years to come?

- Think for a moment of some particularly outstanding success you have had. It could be something personal, in a relationship or in your professional life. It made you feel happy, proud, confident.

- What was this experience?

- What was it made up of?

- How does the memory of that success impact on your attitude now?

CHAPTER V

Inside-Out Alignment

We began by saying that one very effective way of staying happy and in good health is by cultivating and maintaining an inner harmony. We are constantly bombarded by news and information from the media, the chatter of the street and our friends and acquaintances. Most of the time what we hear is bad. The problem is that the information carries its own vibration which we absorb without even realising. Because we are unable to digest this flow or to sort it out so that we only hold onto the information which is useful, our minds are overwhelmed by the hope-less noise of it and we become trapped in a feeling of our own powerlessness. It is deeply destructive therefore, to tune into this one frequency, like a radio station broadcasting round the clock every kind of disaster and atrocity from across the world.

There is another frequency we can tune into, what we could call 'the positivity channel'. This is not about promoting a mindless optimism where everything is for the best « *in the best of all possible worlds* ». The kind of optimism we talking about here is simply a more positive way of approaching things. Positivity does modify our perceptions and helps us see things in a more optimistic way, but as importantly, it helps us first of all, to unify and organize the thinking-acting-feeling subject that each of us is.

In his critique of the structure of language as it became fixed in the West post-Aristotle, Alfred Korzybski noted that « *When we examine our relationships with each other and the wider world we must accept absolutely, that everything is intimately connected, one thing to another. As a result, we must try our hardest to leave aside elemental terminology since it implies an isolation which has no basis in fact.* »

This is the case for words like 'observer' and 'observed', 'body' and 'soul', 'to think' and 'to feel', the 'intellect' and the 'emotions'. We are not simply the totality of those elements either, but much more than that. It makes very good sense therefore to put aside that fragmented, dissociated way of thinking and unify our inner world.

I - Two basic principles

- Principle number 1: positivity is constructive

It is both desirable and possible to visualize success whatever the project, from something as simple as a dish one is cooking for the first time to a radically new idea. It is quite possible to smile at a stranger and help him find his way when he's lost in the city. It is the positive expression of our wishes which leads to action.

The founder of positive psychology, Mihaly Csikszentmihalyi, talks about the « *optimal experience* » as that happy moment when one is fully and unconditionally absorbed in any activity. Such a moment can happen at any time: walking in the countryside, making a meal, washing the dishes, driving one's car, signing off on a piece of work. All that is needed is for the person doing it to be fully present in the moment and wholly engaged in the activity in question. Then there is a concentration of both the head and the heart on the same goal unimpeded by the divisive reasoning mind.

- Principle number 2: The higher level of being has an aligning effect

If we focus our minds on higher things we inevitably see a change in the direction and nature of our thoughts, feelings and behaviour.

When Maslow devised his pyramid of needs, he put self-realization at the very top. Talking about the pyramid of needs at that level refers, of course, less to an idea of things we need to put right or overcome, and more to the impulses and motivations which inspire us and give us the energy necessary to go in a particular direction.

The need to grow

Once the three basic needs have been satisfied (*see Chapter 2*), there is the need for growth. What is meant by that term is the need to develop a responsive capacity adapted to the increasing complexity of situations we are faced with. What we are looking for is new ways of approaching problems, ways of coming together with others to use the strength of a team, and a willingness to tackle projects which will take us right out of our comfort zone.

The decision to take control of our life is critically important in developing an optimism. It is something we come to once we have successfully mastered our dependency on our physical environment, our family and other relationships.

- What new opportunities can you see for yourself right now?

- How do you feel when you think of those?

- How hard would it be to relinquish them?

- What benefits could you hope for in the way of new intellectual, emotional and relational experiences?

- What conditions or limits would need to be in place to enable this project to become a reality?

The need for meaning

Beyond a certain stage of self-realization what we become aware of is a need to work for the benefit of the wider good. We begin to look for ways of handing on our insights and making use of the gifts and skills we have acquired. Solidarity, altruism, involvement in group action, are all important ways of enabling us to contribute and support a cause, humanity, the health of the planet… there is no shortage of subjects. It is generally accepted that altruism and generosity are both psychological and social values which give meaning and structure to the life of the individual.

The process of realizing the full extent of one's possibilities leads one naturally to want to exert some influence over one's environment. There is very little satisfaction to be found in simply settling down and marking time once we have made life comfortable for ourselves. But we must be patient, wait and see what direction we ought to take. We may lack discernment about how we should use our skills and knowledge because we are not sufficiently detached from our own situation. The evolution of each human being is somewhat like opening a scroll and reading the history written there, painstakingly line by line.

If we find we have suddenly lost hope it may well be that it is time to take a new step. If we have lost interest in what we previously loved doing, it may well be that this loss of excitement and engagement contains the seed of some essential next step.

Suppose you are a highly skilled teacher or trainer and you have taught and trained until you have nothing left, you are 'burnt out'. When that happens the ideal solution is to re-fuel, to feed your inner self, to review and renew what you know. If the context in which you work makes that impossible other ways must be found to keep alive your vital strength, your desire for growth. Something new must come of this process. As spring follows winter a renewed sense of well-being always follows a period of aridity. Nothing on earth is constant and time revolves continually, one cycle after another in an endless round.

II - Eliminating discord and incoherence

- Factors which induce disorder

We may feel frightened because we want very much for things to come to pass as we would like them to and yet they might not. We are afraid of the unknown and that makes us pessimistic.

The difficulty of remaining fully in the present moment is by no means the least of our problems. We can easily feel pessimistic about the future – we are very rarely pessimistic about the past or indeed the present! For instance, we can see how the environment is being damaged, we are constantly being told about the alarming rise in sea-levels, pollution, the extinction of ever more species. It is alarming, but we do not necessarily have sink into despair because of it. If we use the information we have to find positive ways of engaging with others we open up a new possibility of acting, of joining with others to become part of the solution.

What part can I play in helping to stem the disasters facing the planet as a result of the growth in human populations? I can certainly reduce how much water I use, and I can recycle, and limit as far as possible the use of all unnecessary packaging. If I do this, I will feel I am participating and that I have some control over my own material life. And an awareness of this type, combined with some kind of action can help keep dark thoughts at bay.

- Fostering beneficial attitudes

Optimism is generated in the mind. What stops it flourishing therefore is a competing activity in the mind, the one which makes it difficult for us to let go. We want to hold onto our attachment to the past, just as we mourn the loss of everything that we remember as good and fine in that era which we believe has gone forever. The remedy consists in taking stock of that past, holding onto the good things it brought us so that we stop constantly looking back longingly and develop a better adaptive capacity to the present moment.

In this regard it is important to remind ourselves that the value of each moment of our life is contained in whatever we are able to express and do **in that moment**. Sometimes we may feel that we have nothing left to give or do, we have reached the limit of our capacities. When this happens it might well be that we have done all we can in that particular area of life. The best thing to do in that case, is to allow oneself some mental 'time-out' and wait patiently for something new to emerge.

- If I feel pessimistic what is it that I am afraid of losing? What am I afraid of no longer being able to do or to make happen?

- What was so important in all of that?

- What did I get out of it that helped me develop (for example, the conviviality and sharing in family gatherings)?

- How can I keep hold of the strength I got from those and use it in other contexts or in other ways?

III - The three points of entry into coherence

The things we cannot will into reality by rational means we can access by other openings, using the affect, action and meditation. Thoughts come with feelings attached and are present before action or one or other kind of behaviour. If one is having difficulty shedding one's dark thoughts, there are other ways of overcoming these.

1 – The affect: Specific values reveal themselves at each stage of our evolution. These values are also a way of expressing different emotions and feelings. The values of inclusion and participation which we find in our earliest stages of development become altruism, empathy, solidarity and even gratitude as we move towards self-realization.

- Make it a rule to think of 3 positive things every evening that make you grateful.

2 – Behaviour and action: If we reach out to help a neighbour or someone we are close to, we feel better for having done so and so does the person whom we have helped. It can be that simple. Remembering this can help make you act in that way when the opportunity presents. One gesture of kindness or love and then another, changes the atmosphere of the world and changes the behaviour of other people. Show kindness because kindness is action. Not only does it have a positive effect on the person to whom it is shown but on the person who does it.

3 – The emotional: We can act on our emotional state at the subconscious level. We can quieten the emotions which disturb us by practising meditation. Allowing oneself to think deeply and quietly in a calm space enables us to step outside the noise of the daily round and tune in to a different frequency, flowing from our inspiration, intuition and our motivations.

IV - Conscience, the X-factor

The philosopher Michel Serres said that 'Logos' – the word, language, reason – was an attempt to find a relationship between disparate things that at first sight have no real relationship with each other. To do this the rational mind has to get rid of everything that unites, all those things living beings hold in common. By putting spirit and soul to one side like this, the reunifying principles end up being relegated to the margins of mainstream society and treated as peripheral religious concerns.

Our conscience is not a physical entity. It cannot be located in one particular area of the brain. It operates in such a way as to open up the possibility for us to find harmony on a more elevated vibrational level. If we turn our gaze inward on ourselves, we can hear our conscience and our intuition speaking to us. Between them they give us information that goes well beyond the limited insights we access in our daily lives. If we can seize the invisible essence we will avoid the knee-jerk reactions of fight or flight, so characteristic of stressed responses. Learning to relax by using techniques of meditation, tai chi or yoga, enables one to develop a quiet strength which makes one able to respond appropriately no matter what situation one is faced with.

 By disengaging from those things which bring either outer or inner confusion and agitation (a huge range of different kinds of pollution in the outer world, strong emotions and stress in one's inner world) and by listening more carefully to one's inner promptings and to what we really need in order to grow and develop, we are following a path that will bring results such that we can hardly dream of.

The case of M. graphically illustrates this point. M lost her job then her husband and had great difficulty in managing her children. One of her colleagues suggested she try meditation. Once M. began to do this, putting herself in touch with her own spirituality, experiencing moments of deep and fulfilling meditation and integration, her world began to change again. She felt a renewed peace within herself. She found work. Her husband returned and her relations with her children greatly improved.

- What aspect have you neglected or forgotten or consciously put to one side (a closer relationship to the natural world, expressing your creativity, enjoying watching your children grow?) because your life 'made' you, because you thought you had 'no choice'?

- What does 'listening to your conscience' mean to you and what would that inner voice say to you?

CONCLUSION

In 'Steps to an Ecology of Mind' Gregory Bateson says the following: « *The royal road to consciousness and objectivity is through language* ». Language is a cultural tool which shapes us and to some extent deforms us in that process. At the same time if we put language to work to help us achieve clarity in our thoughts, we will gain insight into our present situation and see how we might fulfil our deepest hopes and desires.

And beyond words there is a silence which gives us access to a subtler reality. 'Contemplating' a word may be all that is required to reach the deep silence of fulfilment. Likewise, withdrawing for a moment inside oneself and listening to the silent voice of intuition will connect us once again with the invisible. For our conscience is much more than our persona, and we are more than the limited social creatures we so often show to the world outside.

www.ingramcontent.com/pod-product-compliance
Lightning Source LLC
LaVergne TN
LVHW091726190726
843493LV00001B/470